MW01097591

THE HEBREW ALPHABET

Book of Rhymes for English Speaking Kids

SARAH MAZOR
YAEL ROSENBERG
Cover: Raiza Pascual

MazorBooks

ISBN 978-1-947417-20-5

AUTHORS' NOTE

There is a benefit to exposing your children to more than one language: Multilingual-kids have been found to be better at learning, planning, problem-solving, and self-control.

With this Hebrew Alphabet book, you will not only provide your children (and you) with a lifelong connection to the Bible and to Israel, you will also enhance their development.

The Hebrew Alphabet: Book of Rhymes for English Speaking Kids is the first in the MazorBooks series of 'A Taste of Hebrew' for children. Look out for additional books in the series.

Shalom!
Sarah Mazor and Yael Rosenberg

Please note: Though the Hebrew language is read from right to left, this book, which is primarily written in English, is designed accordingly and should be read from left to right.

עברית לילדים
Hebrew for Kids

IN THIS BOOK

- The Hebrew Alphabet Chart
- The Sounds of Hebrew Letters
- Guide to Transliteration of Hebrew Words
- The Hebrew Alphabet in Pictures and Rhymes

More About Hebrew:

- Interesting Facts
- Silent Letters
- A Bit of History: The Ancient and the Modern

THE HEBREW ALPHABET

ד dalet	ג gimel	ב vet	בּ bet	א aleph
ט tet	ח chet	ז zayin	ו vav	ה hei
	ך chaf sofit	כ chaf	כּ kaf	י yud
	ם mem sofit	מ mem	ל lamed	
ע ayin	ס samech	ן nun sofit	נ nun	
ץ tzadi sofit	צ tzadi	ף fei sofit	פ fei	פּ pei
ת tav	שׂ sin	שׁ shin	ר reish	ק kuf

The aleph and the ayin are silent letters.They both take the sound of the vowel that accompanies them. These vowels look like lines and dots that usually appear beneath the letter. The hei too is usually silent when it appears at the end of a word.

The Sounds of the Hebrew Letters

ALEPH sounds like the 'a' in arm*

BET sounds like the 'b' in buttons

VET sounds like the 'v' in vest**

GIMEL sounds like the 'g' in games

DALET sounds like the 'd' in doll

HEI sounds like the 'h' in happy

VAV sounds like the 'v' in violet

ZAYIN sounds like the 'z' in zoo

CHET sounds like the 'ch' in Bach**

TET sounds like the 't' in toy

YUD sounds like the 'y' in yellow

KAF sounds like the 'k' in kite

CHAF sounds like 'ch' in Loch Ness**/***

LAMED sounds like the 'l' in lemon

MEM sounds like the 'm' in mommy

NUN sounds like the 'n' in nursery

SAMECH sounds like the 's' in story

AYIN sounds like the 'a' in alligator*

PEI sounds like the 'p' in play

FEI sounds like 'f' in flower**

TZADI sounds like the 'tz' in pretzels

KUF sounds like the 'k' in kitten

REISH sounds like the 'r' in ribbon

SHIN sounds like the 'sh' in shoes

SIN sounds like the 's' in sky**

TAV sounds like the 't' in television

*As both the Aleph and the Ayin are silent letters, they take on the sound of the vowel that accompanies them. The vowel 'patach' - which sounds like 'aa' - is used in the examples above.

** Alternate sound of same letter (bet/vet, kaf/chaf, pei/fei, and shin/sin).

*** The 'CH' sound is like the noise made when clearing one's throat.

Guide to Transliteration

a: as in barn

e: as in sled

o: as in go

i: as in me

u: as in glue

ei: as in day

tz: as in pretzel

ch: as in Loch Ness
like the sound you make
when clearing your throat

EVERYBODY
COME AND LEARN
THE LETTERS OF THE
ALEPH-BET

START WITH ALEPH
END WITH TAV
TWENTY-TWO THAT
MAKE THE SET

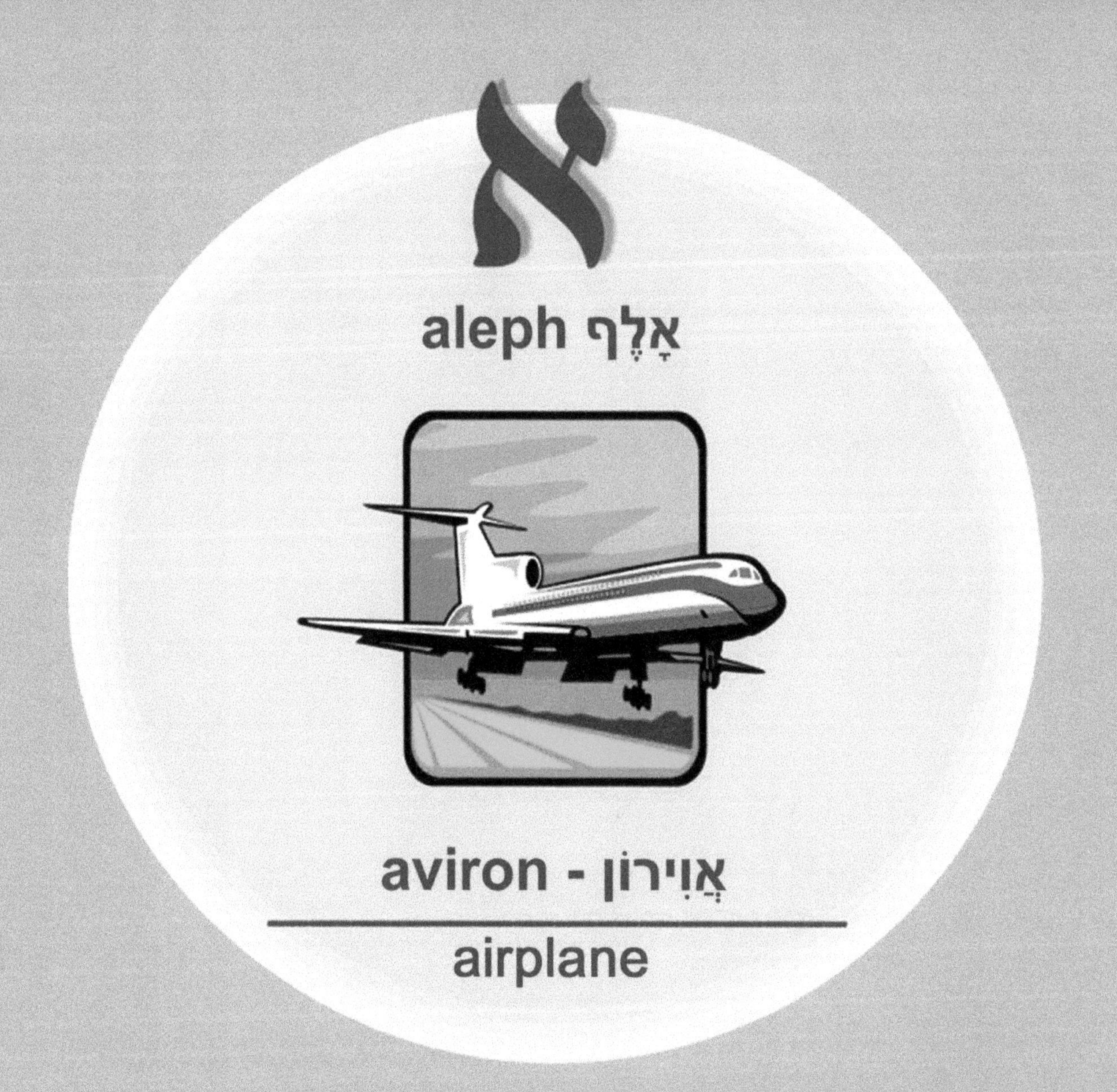

Tiny little Avi wants to fly up high
And from the AVIRON wave to all goodbye

Tiny little Bina plans to sing and act today
With her favorite BUBA in her kindergarten play

Tiny little Gadi loves food that's cold and sweet
He much prefers a GLIDA over any other treat

Tiny little Danny wants his pet to come to bed
Mommy finds a DUBI that can sleep with him instead

ה

hei הֵא

hipopotam - הִיפּוֹפּוֹטָם

hippopotamus

Tiny little Hilla heard a huge noise at the zoo
A HIPOPOTAM with a cold sneezed loudly... *achoo!*

Tiny little Varda who is pretty like a rose
Smells a bright red VERED with her tiny little nose

Tiny little Zevi is really very smart
He separates the pit from the ZAYIT's softer part

Tiny little Chananya likes his pet a bunch
He shares with his CHATUL his breakfast and his lunch

Tiny little Tali loves all forms of transportation
A TRAKTOR ride was on her list to do on her vacation

yud יוּד

yalda - יַלְדָּה

---

girl

Tiny little Yaeli is incredibly mature
She's a 3-year-old YALDA but people think she's four

Tiny little Keren smiled the widest ever smile
When Daddy brought a KELEV home to visit for a while

lamed לָמֶד

leitzan - לֵיצָן

clown

Tiny little Leah likes to dance and sing and play
And dress up as a LEITZAN does every other day

Tiny little Mordechai is almost four years old
A MATANA is wrapped for him with ribbons red and gold

nun נון

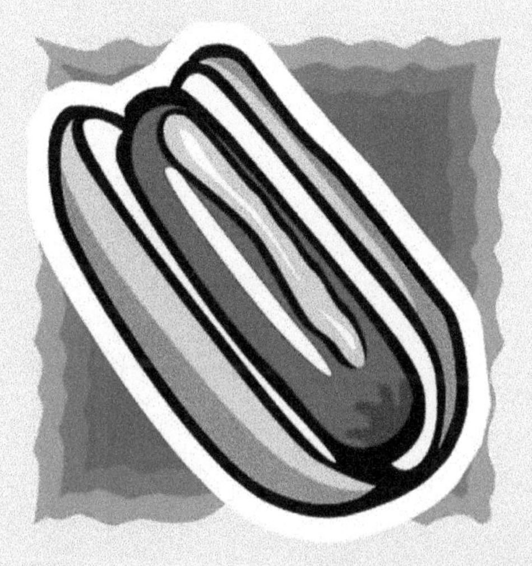

naknikiya - נַקְנִיקִיָּה

hot dog

Tiny little Netanella is the fastest eater
In a NAKNIKIYA contest nobody can beat her

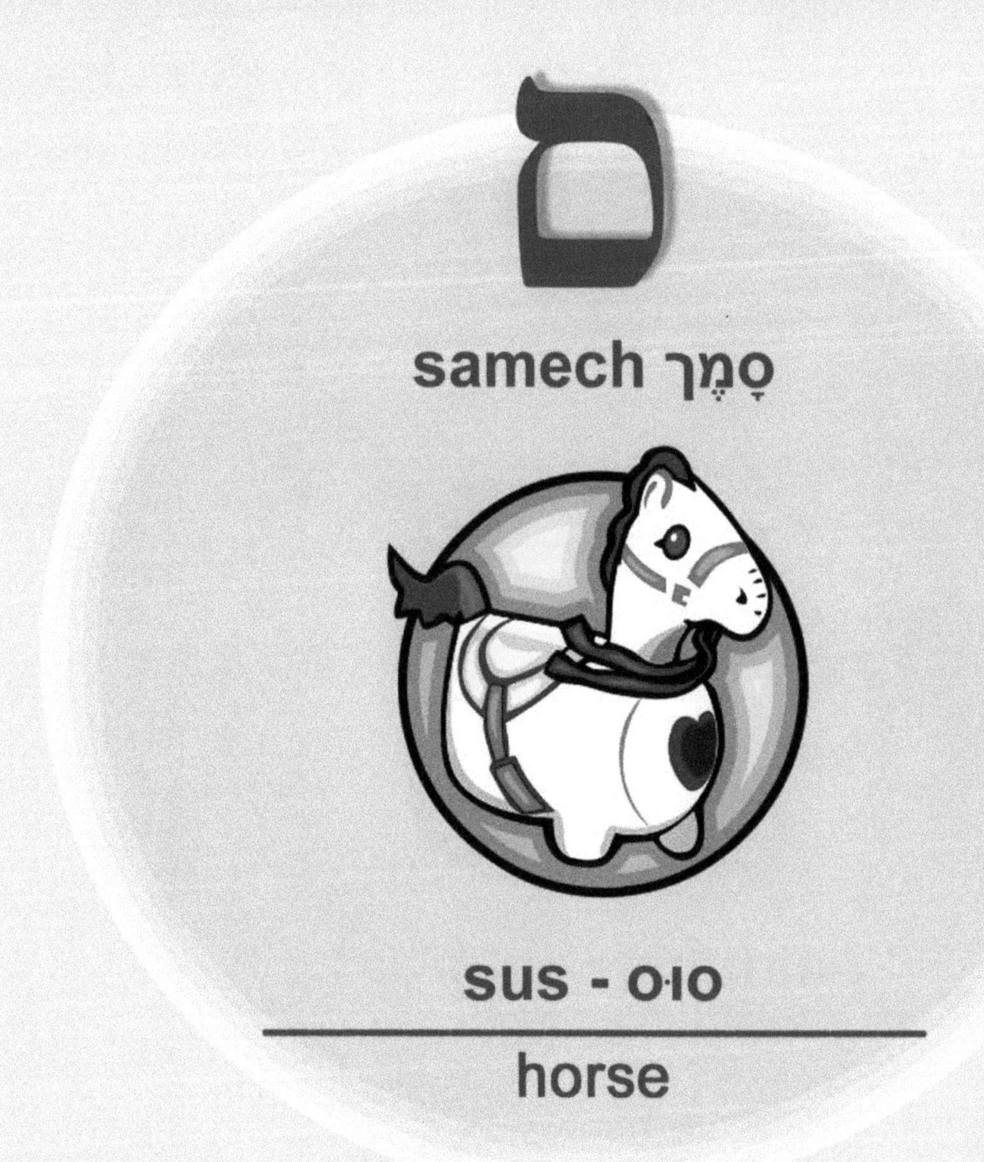

Tiny little Sigalit adores her uncle Matt
Who rides a SUS and on his head he wears a cowboy hat

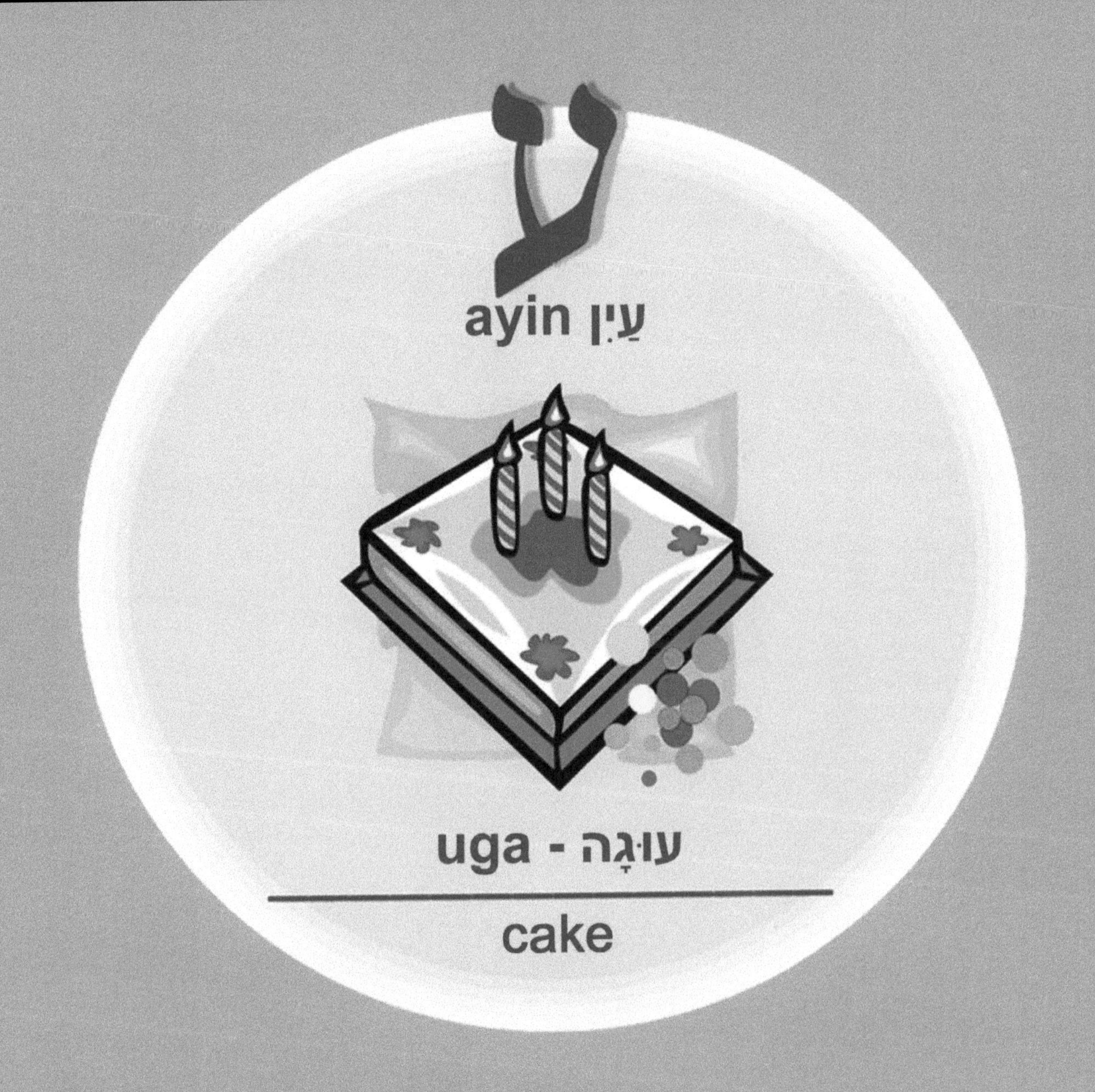

Tiny little Edna is a very gifted girl
She bakes a choclate UGA with some sweet vanilla swirl

Tiny little Pnina has a wild imagination
She dreams of riding on a PIL during her vacation

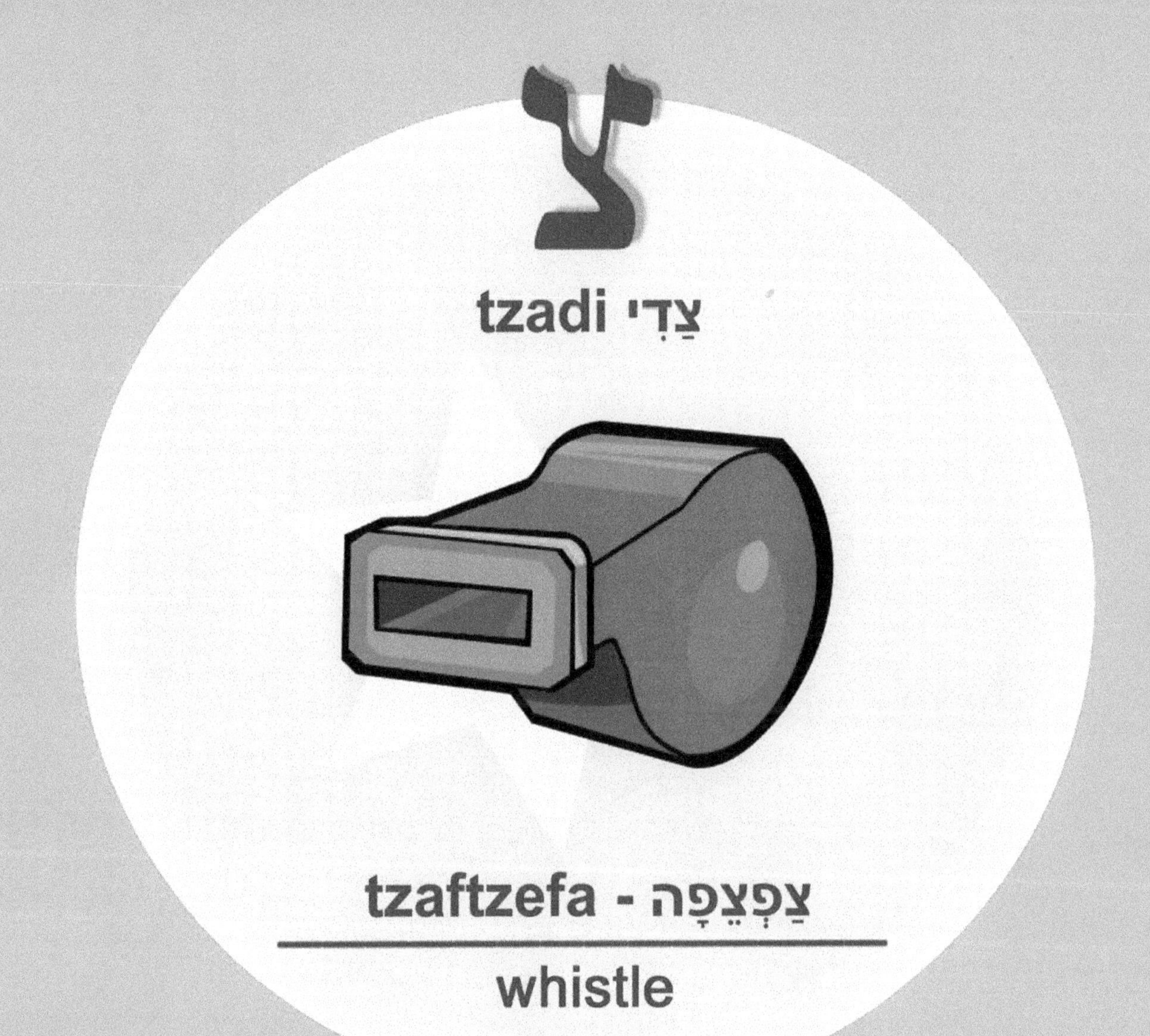

Tiny little Tzippi pretends she is a coach
She blows a TZAFTZEFA when she sees the kids approach

Tiny little Kobi grows different kinds of seeds
He uses his KUMKUM to water plants and weeds

reish רֵישׁ

rakevet - רַכֶּבֶת

train

Tiny little Raphael loves to travel far
He prefers the RAKEVET to riding in a car

Tiny little Shalom loves whenever Grandma Sandy
Brings her bag of SHOKOLAD and other kinds of candy

Tiny little Tami has a heart that's full of joy
Mommy brought a TINOK home - a little baby boy

Hebrew: Interesting Facts

Hebrew is different than English not only in sound but also in the way it is written. The Hebrew alphabet has 22 letters, the first of which is aleph followed by bet. Five of the 22 letters are written a bit differently when they appear at the end of a word. They are the K*af Sofit, Mem Sofit, Nun Sofit, Fei Sofit,* and *Tzadi sofit.* (*Sofit* is from the word *sof,* which means final.)

Some Hebrew letters have more than one sound. For example, the sound of 'P' and the sound of 'F' are represented by the same letter, pronounced *'Pei'* or *'Fei'* depending on the word.

Hebrew vowels are represented by symbols, which generally are not written in texts though they are used in prayer books and beginners' learning books.

The most observable distinction between Hebrew and the western languages is that Hebrew is written and read from right to left.

Hebrew: Interesting Facts, Cont.

The Hebrew Alphabet: Book of Rhymes for English Speaking Kids, the first book in the 'A Taste of Hebrew for Kids' series, focuses on the Hebrew alphabet. In this book, the 22 letters are illustrated and spelled out in English and in Hebrew. In addition to the letters, 22 basic Hebrew words that are appropriate for young children are taught in a fun way.

The words that are selected, one for every Hebrew letter, are written in Hebrew, transliterated and translated into English and depicted with an attractive illustration. Proper pronunciation help is provided with a 'sounds like...' example.

Finally, each Hebrew word included in the book is incorporated into a sweet English rhyme that will help kids and adults recognize the Hebrew alphabet and learn foundational words in this beautiful language.

Have fun learning Hebrew!

Hebrew: Silent Letters

There is only one official 'silent' letter in the Hebrew alphabet, the ALEPH. However, in modern-day Israel the AYIN is regarded as silent by many. The letter HEI is sometimes silent as well.

The ALEPH - א

Words written in Hebrew do not begin with a vowel (unlike English, where vowels are often found at the beginning of a word, as in - 'as' and 'in'). The one exception is the conjunction 'VAV' - as in UGA U'GLIDA, cake, and ice cream. The symbol for the vowel 'U' in Hebrew is 'VAV' with a dot in its belly and when placed before a word it denotes the conjunction 'and'.

When Hebrew words begin with the sound of a vowel, like ADAM, the silent ALEPH is there to hold the vowel. When the ALEPH does not hold a vowel, which occurs in the middle or end of some words, it is silent. For example, ABBA, father, is spelled ALEPH, BET, ALEPH (אבא) - Note that the first ALEPH holds the vowel 'aa' but the second is silent.

Hebrew: Silent Letters, Cont.

The AYIN - ע

Though the AYIN is not really silent, as it does have a sound that also exists in the Aramaic and Arabic languages, most Ashkenazi Jews and a growing number of Sephardi Jews treat the AYIN as they do the ALEPH. Silent. Nowadays it is acceptable to treat the AYIN as if it were silent.

The Letter HEI - ה

The HEI sounds like 'h' in 'honey'. However, when the HEI appears at the end of the word without a vowel, it is silent. For example, the Hebrew word for love is A-HA-VA (אהבה). Ahava is spelled ALEPH, HEI, VET, HEI. The first HEI is pronounced (HA), the second HEI that appears at the end of the word is silent.

Hebrew: The Ancient & the Modern

The Hebrew language, the language of the Bible, was spoken by the Jews of the Land of Israel in ancient times and continued to serve as the language of prayer and study through the generations. The language was revived and reintroduced into the daily life of the Jewish population of Israel in the late 1800s by Eliezer Ben-Yehuda, the father of Modern Hebrew. Hebrew is the official language of the State of Israel.

Modern Hebrew accommodates the advent of societal, environmental, and cultural evolution as well as the new scientific, technological, and new-age innovation. Though Hebrew words are available for modern-day phenomena, English, Latin, and other international words infiltrated spoken Hebrew with words such as telephone, television, or bacteria, to name a few. However, Hebrew language purists are cognizant of the fact that Hebrew words exist for modern innovation and that they are often based on the roots of words that are found in the Bible.

Hebrew: The Ancient... Cont.

For example, the Hebrew word for computer is MACHSHEV. its root of CHET/SHIN/VET is the same for CHOSHEV, a thinker (n.) or thinks (v.). LACHSHOV is to think and MACHSHEVON is a calculator.

Another example: The Hebrew word for train is RAKEVET and for vehicle is RECHEV, both share the root of REISH/CHAF/VET, ride, which is also the root of ROCHEV, a rider (n.) or the act of riding (v.).

The roots REISH/CHAF/VET (רכב)
and CHET/SHIN/VET (חשב)
are Biblical in origin.

(**Note:** The BET and the VET are the same letter as are
the KAF and the CHAF.)

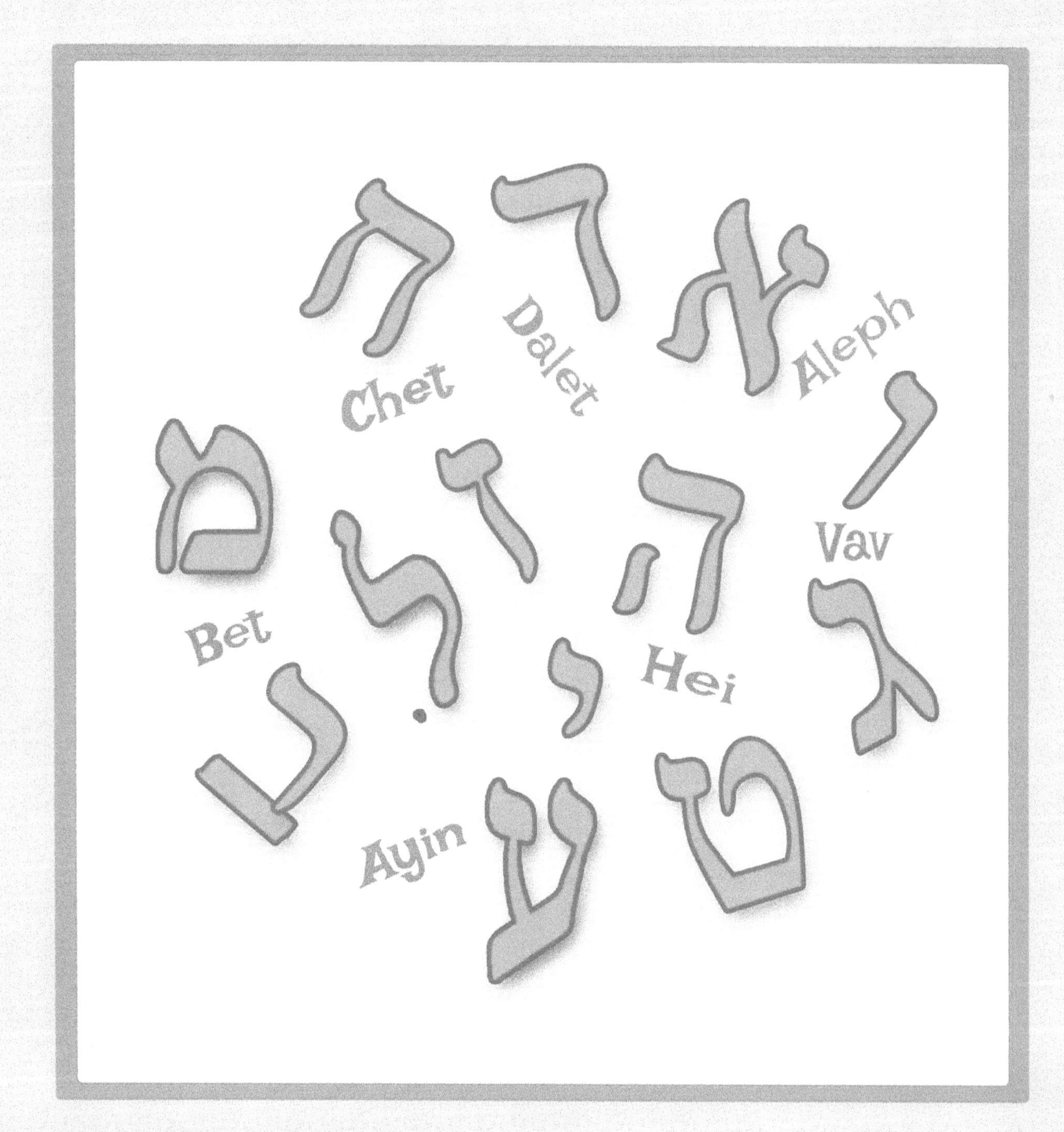
Chet
Dalet
Aleph
Vav
Bet
Hei
Ayin

Check Out the MazorBooks Series

A Taste of Hebrew
for English Speaking KIds

www.MazorBooks.com
www.facebook.com/mazorbooks

שלום
SHALOM